Poems
FOR
EVERYONE

Poems
FOR
EVERYONE

DAVID TALBOT

To order additional copies of this book, contact:
Xlibris
800-056-3182
www.Xlibrispublishing.co.uk
Orders@Xlibrispublishing.co.uk
750509

Contents

Skipping Song 1

Billy's Bungalow Building 2

Growing Up 3

Royal Links - Grouville 4

Deep Sleep 5

To William...7

Aftermath 8

It Beggars Belief 9

Blues For Tam 10

Blues For Belle 11

Megs Pegs 12

Like Lightning 13

Like Thunder 14

Lamb Pooning...15

Liberation..16

Love At First Sight 18

Love At First Sight Pt 2 19

Limerick For A Debutante..20

The Inquisition 21

11th November 2013 22

251204 23

A Musing 24

A Nappy State Of Mind 25

Accessories 26

Across The Way 27

Airport Terminal..28

An Adventure..29

Anon And Anon Sir 30

Aristocratic Cat 32

Disastrous Cat Show 33

Ellaworld 34

Chance 35

Christmas Bliss 36

Christmas Poem 2000 37

Christmas Time 2001 39

Christ's Mass 40

Classical Guitar 41

Close-Shave 43

Cloudburst 44

Dawn 45

Disgrace 46

Dissertation On Desiccation 47

Doubting Thomas 48

Embraceable 49

Dvorak's String Quartet In F Opus 96 50

Etoile 52

E-Volution 53

Father Christmyth 55

Friends 57

Friendship 58

From Here To Eternity 59

From Here To Fraternity 61

Gifts 62

The Golden Eye 63

Gratitude 64

Grumpsies Bananas 65

Handed Down 66

Idylic Lyric 67

If I Don't Love You 68

Imagination 69

Immortality 70

Imperial Mad Dogs 71

Independence 72

In Mimoriam 73

Intro 74

I Am The Lord Of The Dance (Hee! Hee!) 75

It Begins At Home 76

It Takes Guts...77

It Was 78

J.S.Bach Piano...80

Jenny Lake 81

Kismet 82

La Mer 84

Lady Alicia's Bathroom Song...................................85

Magic...86

Mothersday Idyll..87

Railway Walk..89

To Helen 90

The Posh Lady 91

The Black (K) Night 92

Tantrum Dance...94

The Aardvark 95

Night And Day 96

Ode To Anne..97

Ode To Brubeck...98

Parental Responibility 99

Philosophy - Ode To Keats.....................................100

Rebirth...101

Recipe For Success 103

Reflections 104

Reflected In The Window Pane 106

Ships Passing In The Night 107

Siamese Sins..108

Skating On Thin Ice 109

Sleeping Indian 110

The Dreamer...112

Splat...114

Striding On With Pride..115

Summer Snow 116

Talent...117

The Magic Of Christmas 118

The Mystical Wind 119

Under Willow Trees In Summer..............................120

What Is Love...121

Skipping Song

Pee Po Pi Pep
Some little girl better watch her step
Fee Foe Fi Fum
Some little girl better hide from mum.
Washing hands full of soap
She's some hope
For the clothes-lines changed to skipping rope
Pee Po Pi Pep
Some little girl better watch her step.

D. Talbot 1965

Billy's Bungalow Building

They chopped up a tree - Into planks - don't you see
For the roof, the door and the floor. By using an axe,
Sledge-hammer - glass tacks and a singing circular-saw-er.

Windows were made - from the glass - of right grade -
From bottles and jam-jars and glue,
The fire-place from bricks full of kindling-sticks and granpa's pipe for
    a flue.

They created a kitchen - a room for Nan's stitchin'
A bedroom, a bathroom and lounge.
A loft for the pigeon with just a smidgeon and anything else they
    could scrounge.

They made a garden from cement that won't harden
And grass you don't have to mow.
Hours of flowers, daisies - bird-bowers and little drops made out of
    snow.

They changed the roof to a floor in the time you could snore
With tiles and cement all poury
They found a window - a door and a wee bit more
Now - That's another storey.

D. Talbot 31/8/04

Growing Up

Little child skipping happily along
Makes my heart break into song.
Carefree, careless like I used to be.
What has changed me into Me?
Full of fear - frightened as a lamb
What makes Me what I am?
Not long ago
I was free to Grow
Now it's worry and full of woe
Following fashion, fad and cult
Does it mean I've become adult?

15/9/04 D.Talbot
You can't spoil children - Only adults do that!

Royal Links - Grouville

You see them every morning pushing their little prams
The nobody's, the somebody's and the Here-I-Am's.
Their little babies are the irons and the woods
Wrapped up nice and cosy in their little hoods.
The teeing up, the stance, the practise swing
The metallic ting as club meets ball and then takes wing.
The silent curse – the hush is
As terse as a Scotsman's purse
As it lands right in the bushes.
But of Course (strong Irish accent)
It could be worse
It might have been that patch of gorse!
Or mad-scrambles - caught up in barbed-wire brambles.

The time spent by one and all
Looking for that little ball
Seems to be half of the fun
We seek him here - we seek him there
'til half the day is done.
Now here the secret lies - tell not a soul
It was actually spent taking sacrament
In the Nineteenth Hole!

D.Talbot 26/11/10

Deep Sleep

I walk in the sea of tranquillity.
I am over the moon.
The warmth of the sun
Kindling my heart to become sun-like
Pulsing love through my body
Making me alive - vibrant.
At peace with myself
At peace with the world
At one with the universe.
One verse in the poem of life.

I dream in the sky-blue beauty around me.
Beyond thought - beyond being me.
I am part of the green grass
I am the rock that makes mountains
I am the fountain of youth
I am the old man of time
I am the moment of truth
Forsooth - I am everything you see.
The sublime manifestation
Of one's own speculation.

The sea laps peacefully
On the shore
The tide brings more ripples in the sand,
Stippling the patterns it creates with sound
Astounding us with its depth of meaning.
Music lilting and swaying
Laying the foundations of life.
From strife and turmoil
Bubbling, boiling - embroiling us
Into something as tangible as thought?

To comprehend ...
To understand ... actually become.
It's like being cleansed in a shower of rain.
I wake refreshed radiant
Ready to face reality again.

David Talbot 10/2/14

To William

Sombre thought to think upon
REMEMBER THEM
I have forgotten
The Stench of trenches filled with water
Bloated bodies floating - carnal slaughter.
The flower of youth - Expended poppies
Scattered over the battlefield. Their fate sealed.
Blood - Christian Blood - Given to save others?
Against - Blood - Christian Blood - Human Sacrifice?
What Price to pay? Whose Souls were saved?
Those who braved each other?
Brothers in Battle - Each seeking salvation?
Slaughtered like cattle - to feed the nation?

I have forgotten the trenches.
If only I could forget the ashes that remain.
The medals in the drawer I dare not wear
For They that bore the brunt
Out there on the Front
Came back to claim what was theirs.
Mine was the only chest left to pin them upon.
After all I was only doing what I was paid to do
Protecting the Country - from the likes of You?
Cowering in the yellow mud Splattered red by others blood.
How can I wear them with pride when they belong to them that died?
Next time you see a poppies beauty - remember them
That did their duty.

Aftermath

The Heroes of Humanity laid-out.
Little white crosses counting the losses.
Poppies crop up in my garden
Reminders of Flanders.
Squandered Youth - Fathering forth
A gaunt reminder of the past.
Ravished, - Haunted - Taunted even
By the Savagery of War - Devastation
As Solemn as the Somme Psalm
Hymn-Song Psalm Promises
Promises - Promises All Forgotten
Until the next one comes along.
David Talbot May 10th - November 11th 2004

William was my father. A soldier first, a lorry driver second supplying the front line on the Somme. Thirdly he was a cook creating whatever he could from the meagre supplies that he had brought with him, as well as munitions and arms. He was one of The Accrington Pals. Brave Men - Most of them died in this bloody conflict. He was a role model that I have tried to model myself upon. Not very successfully! (He was the best Father I ever had!!)

It Beggars Belief

I am a beggar on the street.
I make my living by deceit.
The leg that's missing is under my seat.
My dog knows, with piteous eyes,
My hat is where his dinner grows
With little sighs and wet nose
He slumps into dejected pose.
He's wise, a better actor than I.
That is why I rely on him
For crowds to toss coins up to the brim.
When my hat is full we call it a day
And have time to rest and play.
I pay my dues to the government
I regard this as money well spent
For if bad times fall
I could claim benefit from the dole.
Not like some who dally all day
And shirk the very thought of work
And haven't paid one jot
Into this governments pot.
My conscience is clear
Many years of war
And fearful scars
Nights spent beneath the stars
Freezing cold, hungry and sore
Not wanting any more
_ I survived - What a diet -
All I want now is peace
And quiet.

David Talbot 10/8/16

Blues For Tam

A flower is for the mind to feed on
To add a little loveliness.
I know lad, I know,
But as you bend your back in the field
And feel the winds caress
Like a fatherly hand ruffling your hair
You lift a little and look for a moment
Down the valley and up to the hill,
Pendle in its mist of peace.
I know lad, I know, It's only a moment
Then back to the toil that's become a pleasure
Because you know
Yes lad you know now
That you are right.
As if your sight's come back again,
And you have time to lift a little
To wonder at a hare-bell in the grass.
I knew a girl once with eyes so blue
As pure as the summer sky.
We wandered down the river valley
And high up onto the hill.
That was the time I saw the hare-bells
Sort of fragile blue like a bird's egg-shell.
T'was then I knew
For I was careful not to tread them down
Like kids missing nicks in the pavement of the town
Now you know lad or at least can guess
A flower is for the mind to feed on
To add a little loveliness.
David Talbot

Blues For Belle

Blackburn Market.
Local voices old and new,
Past and present noises filter through.
Sitting in the sun - outside Marks & Spencers
Where words are spun
Like gossamer cotton.
Less dense in dialect as I remember,
Idioms almost all forgotten
but as warming as the sun.
A few words spoken make more sense
Than a detailed essay could ever have done.

The world is there for us to roam -
Experience life and earn a living
But sometimes life can be so unforgiving
That its nice occasionally to return home.
No matter what
No matter why
The open arms are there
To cry.

D.Talbot. 28/1/98

Note :-They were words not spoken.Rather mouthed - like gossamer
cotton - floating in the mind or mill.Found not by sound but
shape - lips expressing compounded thoughts - Scandal - gossip -
talk of the town - Frowns - Smiles - Love - Doom - Above the
clatter of looms and combs - The warp and weft of fabrication.
Spinning mills filled with poetry -giving the gist.The grist of the
mill to keep them going through the tedium of bringing the bread
home.

D.Talbot 13/2/98

Megs Pegs

The Springbok prancing on the Sveldt
Escaped the Jaws of death
Because the prowling lion smelt
Or had halitosis or bad breath.

This was because he did'nt clean his teeth
Before he went to bed
And all the tartar underneath
The sheen poisoned him to dead.

So - Dear Child - be warned - Take heed
When You are darning socks
And feed your face on apple-pie an mushy-peas
On fizzy-pops and sweeties by the box
On dairy-cream teas an runny honey
Try to remember to clean your teeth
'Cos I'm running out of money

Signed The Tooth-Fairy

Grumps 28th Aug 1904
D.Talbot

Like Lightning

What is a poem?
But a dream
An outlet for the unconscious
Scream in dark
Hidden womb of unknown life.
A preknowledge.

A leap of light like lightning
Looping down the vast void
From thunder-cloud black darkness.

A groaning roar of labouring pain,
A flash .... A cry,
A birth.

A descending peace
Like rain from heaven.

Some labour too long
Instead of the young lion of new life,
Leaping like lightning,
An old deformed crone
Crawls out from the loins.

David Talbot

Like Thunder

It struck me as I gazed, lost haze.
Soft feathers of frost
Crossed on window-wonder of weather.
Low light, blue sky
Midnight-blue at dusk.
Slow lapping clouds crowd
Flow moon-slip silver sapping hue.
Stray beams gleam, alight
Lovely crescent petals, crystal pretty
Delicate, iridescent.

Late frost in frozen glory on the window pane.
Heart beating loud
Mind burst asunder
Emotional pain like thunder
And sobbing rain.

David Talbot

Lamb Pooning

The Gibbons and Baboons
In ribbons and balloons
Were having a hale and hearty.
They had festoons of spoons
Like loony moons -
Star-sparkling, tatty and tarty.

They wanted to attract
Something that they lacked
Like fruit and nuts and tasty-cuts.
So they ransacked
The various shacks
And huts of native mutts
And gave themselves a party.

D.Talbot 23/4/2002

Liberation

(Rejoice! Rejoice! The voice of the People
Ringing out from every steeple)

The Joy of being free from Tyranny
Like a dove being released from the Ark
Rising above the troubled waters
Free and singing like a lark.

A Nation oppressed - Its people depressed.
Freedom should be a right
Not something for which we have to fight.

Only fools
Would vote in a Government that changes the rules
And allowed to control everything
Including which anthem we ought to sing.

The dominated wife, beaten into submission
Finds his gun and ammunition
It takes courage to pull the trigger
And call in the deep grave digger.

The irony
Of the rule of the gun
Is that it could be used for Freedom
Or for Tyranny.

The click of the heels
Echoing down the empty street
The Jackbooted footsteps ....
The missed heartbeat.

We don't want those moments to return
We want an honest crust to earn.
It is only right to see and hear
Our plea. .... Our fear

Is that they don't see our need,
Overcome by personal greed,
Or the love of power.
Sometime soon it will be our hour.

At the end of the day,
Please listen to what we have to say
And understand
After all it IS Our Island.

David Talbot 18/03/15

Love At First Sight

Today
In the cafe
She looked up at me
And smiled.
I looked down
Down into the coffee grains
Of an empty cup,
Fortune-telling.
When I looked up again
She had gone.
I sat alone picking crumbs
Creating a pattern on the cloth
Become a tapestry.
I wrote a pledge
That none but she would understand.
A pledge of love in bread-crumbs
On a dirty cafe table-cloth.
Magic spelling.
Tomorrow
In the cafe,
Of into the scattered
Chair and table forest,
Sheltered from the sun,
She will smile again
And I,
Bursting with love
Will die a second death
And will look down and
Say nothing
For all is understood

David Talbot

Love At First Sight Pt 2

Some fifty odd years later

Eyes meet
And look away
In disbelief.
Shyly
Look again
A smile returned
(Deep sigh of relief).
Not wishing to be spurned
You turn away
And Glance
Eyes dancing
Saying more
Than words could ever do.
Drawing you closer
Till hands meet
And clasp
Something that has always been
Out of your grasp.
A dream come true.

Oh! If only it would happen to me
And You.

David Talbot 26/2/15

Limerick For A Debutante

There was a young lassie called Deb
(Which is a reversal of Bed.)
She was well sprung
He was well hung
Their offspring were very Well-Bred

Sweet young Olivia of Reception
Was a past mistress of deception
She would give you a date
Then tell you you're late
And give you an exceptional inspection.

Dave Talbot 31/5/16

The Inquisition

There was a lassie called Beth
Who chose dentistry instead of death.
The aim of the profession
Is to obtain a confession
Before their victim draws his last breath.

David Talbot 8th June 2016

There was a young nurse called Susie
One
There was a young nurse called Susie
One of her habits was quite boozy
She would fill the Jacuzzi with wine
And with a sanguine sign
Invite you to join her - the floozy.

Dave Talbot 24/05 16

There was a young dentist called Kate
Who intentionally inebriated her mate,
He was a handsome hunk
But as drunk as a skunk,
Then berated him for being in such a state.

Dave Talbot 24/5/16

11ᵗʰ November 2013

Tears fall like rain
Easing the pain.
If there was a god
It won't happen again.
Isn't it odd -
Surely man made god
The inhumanity of war is proof of this.
Instead of bliss
War after bloody war
So rough
Surely god would have said
Enough!

Dave Talbot 11/11/13

251204

Little boy lonely
Bottom of the stair.
Church-mice penniless -
- Cupboard bare.
Christmas is comeing
The Geese are .... obese.
Daddies out shortly on temporary release.
Mummy's out making a Copper or two
I'm doing ...... Fine
How about you?

D.Talbot 11/1/04

A Musing

Somewhere deep in the labyrinth of the mind
Is a secret place - I cannot find.
A haven, a refuge - a Sanctuary
Where peace is graced by love.
I look, I seek, I try to find -
Below - beside and above. I would not mind
But always I seem not to win the right
As if I've lost sight of ....
I'm left outside - never allowed to enter in ... this ...
Moments of bliss - tranquillity - joy forever ... then ...
Everything seems to go amiss.
At last I think I've found the key
To BE
The answer is simply ME.
Unfortunately and this is the sin
When I go to look I'm seldom in!

David Talbot 7/5/2010

A Nappy State Of Mind

There is a beauty here that deeper dwells
Than I can see.
It wells up inside like music
Enveloping all - enthralling ....
Calling ... Calling ... Echoing
Down the halls of time
To where life began
I realise ... that I am
Or I will be
If only I can get out of this bloody pram.

David Talbot 19/1/14

Accessories

The Nile crocodile
With the Wiley smile
Sped through the water with élan and style.
He upset a boat
So the crew were afloat
But only for a little while!
Having had his fill
He slept until
His appetite
Said let's have another bite
Let's go and give someone else a fright.
So he swam and he swam
Right up to the dam
Where he spotted a crocodile hunter.
Having nothing to lose
He began his cruise,
Unfortunately he was a bit of a grunter.
With an accurate shot
He ended up in the pot
And his skin became a handbag and shoes.

David Talbot 22/02/14

Across The Way

(Dedicated to Dennis Duckworth
Inspired by his collage in The New Church Accrington).

The pathway of life has many crossroads
Round each bend is another view
As we progress through its changing modes
There always seems to be something new.

Repetition is one way of learning
Sometimes it seems like we've been here before.
My heart is forever yearning
To become something that I adore.

Whatever it is I hope to find it
Round the next bend or along the next lane.
If I am lucky, forever I'll mind it,
I know my life will never be the same again.

Meanwhile I'll pursue each avenue, road, vale or street
I travel along helping others to be free,
Whilst facing every challenge that I meet
Until I come across the way that I want to be.

David Talbot 7/7/14

Airport Terminal

DEPARTURE

The long drive in the dark
The queue of traffic - nowhere to park.
A journey - inevitably long
I have to go - I must be strong.
So many family and friends
So many flowers, kisses,.farewells
It never ends - Yet there dwells
Above all else - the Love.
The distant view of fells
And then the long, long drive
A life-time waiting to arrive.

ARRIVAL

Trundling runway - Bump and drop
Now airbourne - Heaven non-stop.
I cannot see - The grey enshrouds
and then the Sun - above the clouds.
I am bourne skywards - upon whose wings?
Angelic chorus plays and sings.
Now I know
That this is STOP! Not even slow.
This time I won't be late
Is that Peter?
At the gate?
Sorry mate
I have to go.

D.Talbot 2/9/04
Manchester Departure lounge - Terminal 1
and after take-off

An Adventure

I'm going to write a poem
I don't know what about
I shall churn a few things over
And we'll just see what comes out.
A little sadness is important
To understand how others feel.
Joy, love and kindness
Also add a touch of fantasy
Oh if only - they - were real!
Love is an outgoing power
Oh if only it returned
I wait for over an hour
Only to be spurned.
Meanwhile I sit and wait
For something to happen
That is Fate - everything predestined?
I think if you look further
You will find that it is nothing of the kind.
If I were you I'd go out
And Find out what life is really all about.

David Talbot 20/1/14

Anon And Anon Sir

I am
The unknown
Poet.
You have met me many times
Probably passed by my bones
In the graveyard or kicked the hard stones
Above my unknown tomb.

I have passed through the portal of death
Many times, yet you can still see me.
You can hear my breath as trees sway,
Leaves rustle or birds sing.
Oh yes! You have heard me,
But I - am forgotten
I lie unrecognised, despised even,
All twisted, distorted and rotten.

You, you of this age
Do you still hear the bird-cry
Above the blur of your automobile?
Or does it take the violent rage
Of a storm to make you sigh
And feel the fearful fingers
Tingling down your spine?
Do you whine like a dog at the lightning?

Ah, well!
Linger a little longer.
Come again
But you won't find me, I shall be gone.
Another will take my place.
No, you won't see his face
But you will recognise him - When he's gone.

I see its useless talking.
I - am the unknown
But I - am immortal.
I shall go on walking forever,
Walking through each book
Of poems you care to pick up.
Don't forget me.
Anonymous.

David Talbot

Aristocratic Cat

We are superior in every way
That goes for saying - without say.
Purr Se.
Our servant - the human being
Does our bidding without seeing
How we manipulate
Their fate
Until it's too late
For them to realise
That the wool has been pulled over their eyes.
They obey our every wish
Including tasty morsels in a dish
And when we regard it with disdain
You should see the pain
They feel
It's so real
But do not worry
We don't feel sorry
We expect something better.
Next time you try to whet our appetite
With something pleasant to taste and bite
Do have the sense
(We grace you with our presence)
To pay respect
With the best tit-bits you can confect.

David Talbot 16/5/14

Disastrous Cat Show

I think my owner can forget
The best behaved cat Rosette.
How was I to know
That the tabby I tried to mate
Belonged to the organiser of the show!
It's too late to change all that
After all I'm only a cat.
The future seems a little more than foggy
Purrhaps our offspring could win next year's 'Best Moggie.'!

When you come 'bottom of the pile'
Put on a smile and if you are bottom of the class
Just wriggle your ass
It's just possible you might win
The best Cat ass Trophy!

David Talbot 16/5/14

Ellaworld

A Fantasy? - Puss-in-Boots?
I coud'nt give two hoots
But if you could choose -
Your shoes, your hose, your clothes
Who's to know what gear you'd wear?
Next time They stare or rear They're glare
At you're apparel
Have they got you over a barrel
Of stout or beer? I doubt or fear
That they could seam or appear to dream
One half as much as you can See.
Staged - perhaps caged - withinThis World
What Ought to Be -This World that Could -
Should become - The Hive-Hum-Happiness of Bliss
Instead of a World - Like This!
If only They would give It a chance
One Glance of Happiness -They would realise
That Paradise is within the eyes
Of Anybody that can see That the only way to be free
Of Fear and Misery is to laugh at Them
That chose to wear Protective Clothes.
A naked thought is more suggestive
Than a digestive biscuit
If only people would care to risk It!

Dear Ella - You were
What others Care to seem
You were not Fantasy or Dream
You dared to be just You
And carried it off
As others would have loved to do.

David Talbot 1/12/04

Chance

At a glance
Most things seem to happen as if by chance.
A close encounter -
Coincidence?
Sometimes we don't know
Which way to go
Which path to take
Which choice to make
Should we say yes
Or maybe no!
I don't know
But I'm one of those
Who prefers to follow one's nose
Intuition - instinctive guess
(And usually end up in such a mess)!
If all else fails
Toss a coin and wish for tails.

David Talbot 23/1/14

Christmas Bliss

Cradled child, dreaming deep.
Parent's happy that their babe's asleep.
Maybe someday he will become
Someone capable of fulfilling their dreams.
Making the whole World better than it seems.
Dream on dear child and visualise
The reality beyond the skies
Dream and sleep and realise
That within this World there lies
A Place of happiness.
That's where you are -
Cradled in your mothers charms.

Starlit night blessed with peace
Away from harm and ceaseless strife
Who could want for a better life?
The beauty and blessing of a Christmas morn
The perfect time to be born.

David Talbot 30/8/15

Christmas Poem 2000

The hollies berries, the robins breast
As red as the sun in evening's rest.
Fir trees - foliage - chlorophyll
Lettuce leaves, cabbages - colour of dill.
Basil, thyme - asparagus
Vegetables, brassica's as green as grass
The sky is the colour the hue is blue
The question is which colour are you?
Mistletoe berries as white as snow
Or - night the lack of light
Dylan Thomas - bible black.
Purple, magenta, indigo
Elderberry, cranberry, blackberry, sloe
Yellow, orange, tangerine-glow
Rose-hips, syrup - candlelight
Flickering between black and white.
Shadow, dark-dawn and bright Caen
Sea - colour - oceans - where life began.
Fluid form and shapes emerge
And life itself is on the verge
Of becoming real
As things start to touch and to feel
Tentacles linger - cling and grasp and grope
Every aspect, hope - and fear that rears its head -
Fodder for the living dead.
Predators, parasites - life on life.
Strife and turmoil not much fun
Nothing is possible without the sun.
People worshipped the source of life
Even to the point of sacrifice.
Aztecs, Incas - cultures gone -
Vultures feeding on the bones -

Alone - with our thoughts -darkest night.
A rainbow - prism - spectrum of light
Illuminates the path ahead that awaits
Star bright or is it really as dark as Fate.
D.Talbot 22/2/2000

Christmas Time 2001

Christmas is a time to give.
Christmas is a time to forgive
The pettiness of others.
Christmas is a time to give
Time for thought
Time for others - thoughts.
Maybe the pettiness was ours.
Maybe there is something
In Christmas after all
When you think about it.
Christmas is a time to give
Thanks.
A Thanksgiving.

D.Talbot
Sept/oct2001

Christ's Mass

Tinsel-stars - reflecting light
From one pure candle burning bright.
Flickering, scattering and dancing about
As the windowing wind tries to blow it out.
Life hangs in a breathless hush
Like morning dawning -
Song of thrush – longing.... yearning.....
The Earth gives birth with Joy and Mirth
A Boy is born - we have a son.
The Rites of spring
Bringing us back to a Beginning
The fading Sun tells us that the Day is done
Deflected light turning darkness into Night
The Earth turns - creaking Space -
Burning friction - The Human Race
Evolves, revolving round at an astounding pace.
If only we could understand that this is the promised-land
The very Joy of Man's desiring.

It's a shame about the wiring
The tree on fire - the lights burnt out
Casting more than a shadow of doubt on Christmas Eve
Just what is it that we do believe?
Dave Talbot 24/9/03

Classical Guitar

Fretful fingers playing a round
The kneck of a guitar. Sounds
Carry me off to distant lands afar.
Instant coffee - Brazilian
Mexican tortilla - tequila - Villa -
Ravishing Spanish fandango -
Flamenco - Tango -
Colourful swirl of Matador cape
Skirts of girls dancing
Picador horses prancing
Escapes
Into whirling wings of birds -
- Paradise - spice
Tropical parrots – macaws
Preening feathers with beak and claws.
Herds of wildebeest
Strumming hooves
Africa - The Middle East -
Mona lisa in the Louvre.
Jamaican rumba, South African samba.
Indian Squaws aquiver
Arrows as straight as the river
Nile - Crocodiles jaws agape.
South African grape
From the Cape.
Plectrum Spectrum
Spectacular display
Virtuosity plucked from the air
Such flair and talent
Taking away want and Care.
D.Talbot 8-10 July 2004

If only I could play like That
I would flay that bloody cat.
To have It's guts for my guitar
So that I would become a Star
Like Ravi Shanka on the sitar.

Close-Shave

Daddy looks so funny
All lathered up in soap
I hope he doesn't cut himself
I don't want him to mope
Like a bear with a sore tooth
And with a strip of sticking plaster
He would look so uncouth,
Another shaving disaster.
But doesn't he look funny
His face all smeared
All white and frothy
Like a Father Christmas's beard.
The razor is a cut-throat
Whittling down his chin.
I can't take my eyes of him
My grin is changed to grim.
I feel so afraid
At the sight of that sharp blade.

Now my big brother he's a modern man
And takes advantage of this age
Whenever he can.
He very rarely cuts himself
And shaves himself so clean
With that modern, little electric
Mowing-machine.

David Talbot 17/2/66

Cloudburst

Alice by the lake, crying.
Mind mixed up? - Thoughts of folks dying?
Morbid thoughts at least.
Gripping tears in the throat
Clinging coldly to her wet coat and sighing
For some sad unreasoning fear.

Drear weather, rain and wind.
Unkind words from someone dear?
Or some self-unforgivable sin?
Seek, O seek a reason Alice
Child, but, no it comes from deep within.
Inexplicable sad despair; no malice.
Hopeless mess like tangled hair.
Some slight relief; sobbing tears
Not quite like grief.

David talbot

Dawn

Morning has broken
My heart,
My mind, cannot find
a more fitting token
Than the rising sun
Carrying your smile,
Your gift to others
Making life worthwhile.
You loved
You gave
The warmth of life
To all and left us
With the Grace
of your memory.
Thank you.
David 19/2/2003

Disgrace

The sheer joy of rain on my face
Washing away tear-stains
Of fear and pain - relief - release.
Moments of peace - space
To move on and accept the fact
That there are things in life that I lacked
With grace.
Will I ever learn to discern
Good from bad?
Will I always be had
By those that chose a life of crime
Swindling others for every dime that they can get?
It is one lesson I shouldn't forget
Apart
From the one
That stole my heart.

David Talbot 10/9/16

Dissertation On Desiccation

When it comes to good desserts and puddings
That really set the taste-buds budding,
Coconut-milk as smooth as silk
Takes some beating
When it comes to really treating.
It's nice with rice
But there's something phoney
When it's mixed with macaroni.
Coconut itself, when finely milled
And mixed with its milk - then chilled
To make ice-cream
Creates a dessert that is a dream.
It's the desert bit - the dehydration
That brings forth this desertation.
Without any if's or buts'
What a way to desecrate your nuts!

Dave Talbot 18th Feb 2016-02-28

Doubting Thomas

I was brought up to believe.
Dear Father
I know your belief
Helped you to bear the wear and tear of war.
Scared, scarred, probably frightened beyond death
You carried on not caring whether it was your last breath.
Doing your duty for the freedom of mankind.
Finding energy beyond self
In Giving - given unto.
Belief. A moment's relief.
I know your belief was real
But do you know how I feel?
Unsure - not knowing which way to go.
I haven't got your trust
I could believe - if I must
But
My word is my sword
Why do I have to trust in The Lord?
Why Don't I just trust?
Myself?

David Talbot 4/9/16

Embraceable

There was a young lassie called Tracey
Who loved wearing things quite lacy
Without a word of a lie
She's as straight as a die
But sometimes can be quite racy!

Dave Talbot 23/11/14

Dvorak's String Quartet In F Opus 96

(American) 2nd movement

Where do you go when you fall asleep?
Do your dreams help you to know?
Sometimes the depths are ever so deep
They are so dark there is nothing to show.
There is such a sadness hidden there inside,
Deep down beyond the tide,
Beyond the moon's influence -
If only?

That is life - Harsh brutal reality.
A dance to the death -
Or a breath of life?

Remember the moments of joy
Never forget.
Recreate those moments
Never regret.

Dance - dance my darling
Through my dreams.
Make me remember life
Is not always as it seems.
Let me recall and try and create
That joy and bliss before it's too late
And the moments missed.
Death comes too quickly for those that wait
I shall not wait for fate to catch me -
I shall dance - dance with you my darling

Through my dreams.
It is one dream I shall never break.

Maybe they will play this at my wake.

David Talbot 29/5/16

Etoile

Tribute to Eric Satie
(Read slowly)
Light
In Darkness
Black in white
Contrast
Inkling
Colour twinkling
Dolour
Sadness ...... lasting
Into ... night.
Star.....tling
Sin.....king
Hope.....ing
Sub.....merging.
Chrysalis
Emerging
Imago
Flight
Light as loveliness
Like delight
As soft as kindness
Kindling love
Life.

D.Talbot 29/7/12

E-Volution

There was a time
When time was not.
Nothing was going on.
It was as if everything had been left to rot
In the warmth of a dying sun.
If a sun was dying
And things were rotting
Then something must be stirring
Maybe forgotten and woe begotten
But nevertheless - occurring.
Evolving – revolving
Casting light and dark
And in the flickering of an eyelid
Creating the elusive quark.
That little bit of matter
An article called a particle
But it doesn't seem to matter.
The top and bottom of it is
That the ups and downs in life
Strange though it may seem
Have a charm of their own.
As if in a dream
Auntie Quark took a walk in the park
And in a roundabout way
Began to sway to and fro
Like a pendulum - So
Time came into being.
When life began the beat of the heart
Was the rhythmic clock
The tick-tock of time
And was only recognised when man became aware
That day and night evolved with the sun
Going round the earth
And then realised it was in reverse

The earth went round the sun
Back and forth the tide rose and fell
Under the sun and moon's gravitational spell
Where we go from here only time will tell
But I can tell you this in rhyme
It will take time -
Probably a life-time.

David Talbot 19/1/14

Father Christmyth

Footprints from the fire-place
Just about daddies pace?
No - it couldn't have been him
He's neither lean or slim
Enough
To climb down with all that stuff.

The half-eaten pie
The glass of wine
The pie was good but the glass of wine
Was only fit for feeding swine!
Imagine in each house - a bite - a sip
You'd be full to bursting - what a trip!
It does explain why Santa's fat and jolly -
Too many pies – that's his folly.
Although really I can't see mummy -
With Big-Fat-Tummy -
Imagine - mistletoe-kissed-
Waltzing with him to Brahms & Liszt!
Christmas morning
Fancy-Wrapping-Paper adorning
The floor - the fun and dancing - prancing galore -
And it's only just begun -
Lots of kids having fun -
What can I say -
It is what makes Christmas Day!
Footprints in caster-sugar-snow
It just goes to show
Who believes it you or I?
I don't know!
But that is why
We strive

To keep the Christmas Myth alive
Although hidden by the snow
The little bit of reindeer sh...!!
Was really overdoing it
D Talbot 24th Oct 2000

Friends

I would just like to thank you all for having put up with
my oddities and occasional bad manners for which I apologise.
One thing I am going to miss most over the next few weeks is
the pleasure of your good company, which I treasure.
Being with you here at Dao yin has been a revelation - as to how
or why
is beyond thought or words, but there is something ... something
special.
In consequence ... well I'll let the poem speak for itself

Friendship

A bond
That does not tie one down.
A hand to hold in trust,
Without a frown.
A shoulder to cry on if you must.
Someone who will be there if needed.
Someone who doesn't mind
If their advice goes unheeded.
Take care when making friends
For if it comes to bitter ends
Be sure that You care,
For if needed
They will be there,
To share
Whatever, whenever ....
It seems a shame
That when you can't do the same
And don't know what it's all about,
Never - doubt
And
Be assured
That they will understand.

David Talbot 9/6/14

From Here To Eternity

Life is a journey we all have to tread
And when you stop walking it - you end up dead.
Now is that the end - is there no more
Or do we carry on to a distant shore?

The answer to this we will never know
Up to the time we have to go.
When we have gone will we find out?
What this mystery is all about?

I have no answers; the answer is there beyond the pale.
You might find out when you set sail.
Meanwhile let's get on with this life that we've got
Making the most of it - until it is not.

Caring for others helps pass the time
And as an extra bonus it will keep us from crime.
Life is roundabouts and swings
Giving and taking amongst other things.

Life and Time like the moon and tide
Are tied together - hand in hand - side by side.
We started this journey with nothing but gifts
From our parents our heritage and that which uplifts

Us into the beyond. Beyond our self, beyond being me
So that we can hear and see
The inner voice - if only we did heed
It would probably give us everything that we need.

To get us through this life and maybe beyond
But I'm not a fairy with a magic wand.
All I can say is make this life worthwhile
By being yourself and putting on a smile.

Setting an example to the young and needy
And most of all stop being greedy.
Helping others as much as you can
Will certainly make you a better man.

Well after all this chatter
Getting to the next world shouldn't really matter
The past has gone - you can't bring it back
Oh! If only I had the knack!

The elusive future might happen somehow
But what really matters is Here and Now.

David Talbot 28/1/15

From Here To Fraternity

An only child is a lonely child.
Happiness depends on making friends.
Acquaintances come and go
Friendships mature ... oh, so slow
That one tends to depend on so called friends
Only to find that they can be so unkind.
Someone you called a mate
You suddenly become to hate
Even despise
Oh if only I could fraternise.

David Talbot 15/1/14

Gifts

Christmas is a time for giving
Christmas is a time for living.
Christmas is a time for spending
Which goes on - never ending.
Buying in for the feast
Lots of goodies - feed the beast!
We are told to remember that
Before the end of september
Christmas is coming the 'geese' are getting fat.
Order Now (smell a rat?)
We are coerced - presents, cards, wrapping paper
What a caper buying now - paying later.
Why? - because were expected to
Because its what we always do
You give me - I give you!

There are some that create
Things beautiful to behold
To listen to - to be told -
To sing and dance and merriment -
Things we'd say are god sent.
It's a strange world in which we live.
- Our vision lifted -
The ones that give
are they gifted?

D.Talbot 18/9/98

The Golden Eye

Ankle deep in the receding tide
Sun on my back
I peer wide-eyed
Amongst the wrack
And the darting fry
For the ever elusive Golden Eye.
It's a new world that you look upon
Now you see it - then its Gone!
The mysterious glint
Of reflected light,
Like twinkling stars within the night,
Draws you - magnetic -
Within it's power,
to keep you out there
For more than an hour.
It's when you peer into those eyes,
That seem to hold you - Hypnotise -
Until you reach out and drag
One more cockle into your bag.

23/6/93 David Talbot

Gratitude

My glass was empty
You poured me a drink.
My mind was empty
You made me think.
My arms were empty
You filled them with warmth.
My heart was empty
You filled it with Love.
Before I met you
I was a hull,
My life was empty
Now it is full.
Thank you.
D.Talbot. 20/3/96

Grumpsies Bananas

Nana the octopus was lolloping along
The bottom of the Sea
He scoffed a kipper
And a little nipper
Before he came up to me.
He said "Hello" and bit my toe
Then scuttled of in glee.

It became quite dark
And then a shark
Loomed out of the murky water.
He said "Hello"
Which way did it go?
One minute more - I'd have caught her.

It became surreal
When a seal
Revealed a chest -
A Pirate's nest
Full of silver and gold.
Coins and gems,
Goblets, crowns and ever sparkling diadems
All from the days of Old.

A cloud came by
I wondered why?
And then a clap of thunder.
It pelted down!
I would have drowned
If I had'nt been down under.

D.Talbot 31/8/04

Handed Down

The earth muffled
In white polar-bear fur,
Warm – hibernating -
Waiting for things to occur.
Silent as the stalking frost
Time steals by.
Too late to turn back the clock
Frost-locked sea – sealing the fate
Of those that chose
The skill of killing to survive,
One way of keeping the body alive.
Striving against all odds
Even the will of early Gods,
The will of old,
To unfold further tales
As yet untold
Of those that failed.
The history of mankind is developing
Future glory enveloping all
In life's ability to appal.
The tale is tolled
Death-knell falling on deafened ears
Recalling all those lost years
Frozen in silence
By the relentless cold.
Listen to the glistening sound
Of voices past – yet still profound.

David Talbot 11/1/05

Idylic Lyric

We met on a moonlit night
The receding tide leaving silver strands of reflected light.
Undulating ripple patterns scattered across the sands.
We walked hand in hand
Feeling for the future of each other.
A moment's grace of being one
Then it was gone
Like clouds drifting across the moon
Cutting out the sun.
There was silence except for the distant murmur of the sea.
Finger touching tenderly
Sensing what had gone wrong
Longing for the song of love to return
Yearning to be together
For ever - a want - a need to be one.
To carry on as if nothing had happened.

Listen to the lapping of the distant tide
Music - accompanying rhythm - to hearts beating as one.
The soft hand in mine gently sensing - reassuring that all
Was not lost that we could carry on caring and sharing our love.
The moon looming out from the shrouding clouds
Showing us our way forward together across the sands
Into the sea of life.

David Talbot 20/3/13

If I Don't Love You

(David's Classical Choice 28
Dorothy Shore pi, vcl)

Piano keys like a harp
Plucking at your heart strings
Bringing a declaration of love.
"Listen ... My Darling
If Music be the voice of love
Play on ... Let me sing ...
Listen to my song ... of longing,
Take my hand,
If I don't love you,
If you think I don't love you
Then you will never understand".

David Talbot 18/9/15

Imagination

We enter make-believe and find
That we have left ourselves behind.
I can pretend to be
Anybody - I'm fed up with being me.
I want to be famous and refined
Become a star - by far the best
Somebody better than the rest.

Clip-clopping along in mummy's high heels
I know now just how it feels
To be a lady wrapped up in mink.
I won't even have to think -
Now there's a thought
Everything that I've been taught
Has come to nought!
It don't make sense,
An insult to my intelligence
It makes me wild
If that's being adult
I prefer me as a child.

David Talbot 13/8/16

Immortality

Whilst you're alive
Strive to do something,
Strive to be someone.
It's your only chance
Before you dive
Into the abyss
Of Nothingness,
Last breath
And do the dreadful
Dance of death.
That is why
You should do something
To be remembered by.
Leave your mark
Before you transit into dark.

David Talbot 30/8/15

Imperial Mad Dogs

The cricket season is over summer has just begun.
It's been raining for the last six weeks and now we've got the sun.
It's been teeming down like cats' and dogs' filling all the brooks.
Not very good weather for cricket but perfectly all right for ducks!
With all the things that have been said you could knock me down
    with a feather
You can't believe half of the things that are being blamed upon the
    weather.
British Rail they are top of the list with excuses for being slow
"Wet leaves upon the track "and "Its' the wrong type of snow"
If you are a foreigner in England and don't know what to say
Just talk about the weather and you will be okay.
Whether or not we like it whatever we do or say
The good old English weather will have its' part to play.
The resilience of the English is recognised World Wide
If it is sport, war or whatever they'll want you on their side.
It is our typical English character our national temperament.
Its' the way we get on with it no matter what is sent,
Whatever is thrown at us we take it on the chin
No matter how tough life is we face it with a grin.
We'll battle through - Whatever the future will bring
Because if you can put up with the English weather
You can stand up to anything.
David Talbot 19/10/11

Independence

I was sleeping deep in dreams
When I heard horrendous screams.
In reality it was the creaking door
(Do remember ... I am only four),
But the thought that some ... thing was coming in
Creepy-crawly - prickly skin -
I panicked ... I held my breath
Certain of approaching death'
I tried to shout
I must have simply - passed out
Of sight
For I shouted with all my might
But no one came to my aid
Which is a shame - Cos' I prayed and prayed.
Maybe they were all delayed,
Mummy, Daddy even god.
It may sound odd
But now that I know I'm all alone
I know I can make it on my own.

David Talbot 19/1/14

In Mimoriam

You can only mourn the dead.
The living you can love.
For all the words that have been said -
The olive branch and dove.
The deeds are done
The times have gone
And now she is above
In peace
Thank God.

5/1/2001
D.Talbot.
To a sister I never met
But would have loved to.

Intro

On Behalf of Tina, myself and our group I Would like to take this opportunity of welcoming Newcomers into our circle. I hope you find the peace and tranquillity that dwells within all of us and that communal being together that we all need.

I normally take Meditation on the last Friday of the month - like today. I usually read a poem which may stimulate a starting point for your meditation, followed by some music conducive and complementary to the poetry.

Actually I think most of us have a quick kitten-nap or thirty winks!

Today is going to be different. Music and Dance have always been part of our heritage - Dance is inborn - The Rhythm of the heart-beat - the lapping of the tide - the music in the wind - Bird-song - the voice rejoicing in the ability to communicate.

Ritual has been the coming together of people to share and Joy in being together. I have been going through my collection of recordings for some time now and going through relatively early traditional Jazz I came across more than a few classics - I was dancing to them instinctively - Joying in being alive - vital! - being part of what I strive to be in meditation.

Rhythmic movement - Dance - is a form of meditation. If you can or care to when the music starts I hope you will feel the influence and join in. Otherwise I do hope you find something in the music that is uplifting and gives one a sense of being alive.

I Am The Lord Of The Dance (Hee! Hee!)

Rhythm and beat
Dancing feet
Trad Jazz Music Oh! So sweet.
Sheer enjoyment moving along
Adding "e"motion to this song.
"Swing Out" baby
"Sweet Kale Rot"
Feet treadin' steps they'd almost forgot,
Eyes all sparkling, sideways glance
Creating the sheer joy of dance.
Oh! Come on Honey get on your pins
Give it a few twirls an' spins
It don't cost money to get rid of your sins!
Come on Baby - Dance and Jive
Come on show us that you're still alive.
Oh Yes! We all can prance
But oh what a joy it is - to Dance!

16/5/15 David Talbot

It Begins At Home

Snow is falling
Like a fragrance from heaven.
Fragile - gentle - delicate.
Each flake is pristine - crystalline - different.
Artistic creations frozen in time for a few moments.

It is snowing
The snowmen are coming
It is snowing
The children are coming
With carrot-red noses, coal-black eyes
And frozen hands to build you.
They will wrap their scarves
Around your necks to keep you warm
And guard you from all sorts of harm.
Snowmen dancing through the night
Sheer delight a proper snowball without fight.
How long will it be before you disappear?
Where do you go to until next year?

It is snowing
Christmas is coming
With pantomime dames and Nativity plays,
Toys galore and mistletoe sprays.
I will give presents - goodwill - create hilarity.
One thing I cannot give - full stop. Is charity
I can't even find it in a charity-shop!

David Talbot 10/10/11

It Takes Guts

Hunting Python was in luck
Grunting Pig becoming stuck.
Trapped between fallen trees
Roaring Lions ignored his pleas
And tore his acheing flesh apart
Each one fighting for his heart.
They ripped and rived and swore
Blaspheming wildly covered in gore.
They gorged and ate and tried to mate
Each appetite to satiate.
Eventually full and satiated
They found each one was overrated.
As Monty began his creep
All the Lions fell asleep.
Now Monty the Python could not hide
The hollow feeling he had inside
And craved that he could fill
This gap - this Gaping Gill,
But no matter how much he tried
He found it hard to swallow his pride.

D.Talbot 30/9/04

It Was

It was Christmas Eve in the workhouse
The money had just run out
Any form of festival fun
Was cast very much in doubt
But the workers remained undaunted
They'd been through a lot worse than this
Being penniless, hungry and homeless
The workhouse was sheer bliss.
Giving shelter - some warmth and company
To anyone that turned up at the door.
When you're done on your heels
You don't know how it feels
To be given food, shelter and more.

They went off to the woods and found kindling
Branches and a few more logs
Their feet were kept warm and away
From harm by the wearing of the clogs.
They also found holly and mistletoe
To decorate the workhouse hall
Then a decision was made by the musicians
They decided to hold a Ball.
The town council and mayor were consulted
They also visited the shops
To provide food, wine and delicacies -
For security they called in the cops.
The event was so successful
They thought that their worries were over
They'd money in hand - it was the Promised-land
All honey, nectar and clover.

This was all well and good but it was to no avail
It was approaching midnight when they found out
That the workhouse had been put up for sale.

There was nothing they could do about it
Except accept the fact
That they were now homeless and - well -
That everybody had been sacked.
Now it wouldn't be Christmas without
A good ending to this tale
If you know one please tell me
Because in this I think I will fail
It looks like I'm heading nowhere
I have come to a full stop.
Well let's be frank with a loan from the bank
They could possibly own their own Co-op.

David Talbot 16/7/12

J. S. Bach Piano

(Goldberg Variations)

Listening to Bach is like watching raindrops falling
Breaking into coronets of beauty - rainbow splashes
Sparkling, startling ones realization into recognising
The necessity of rain - its essential relationship
With Life - as it disappears down the drain.
Then springs back up again.
Germinating, engendering, conspiring
Creating plants to boldly grow into -
Flower-blossom bursting into something beautiful to behold.

Listen, listen to the sun whispering words of love and warmth
Inspiring things to grow and us to know
That forward is the way to go into this world,
This nucleus of beauty allowing us - hopefully
To become part of the whole.
The integrity of a universal identity.

David Talbot 8/12/14

Jenny Lake

Dedicated to Jackson Hole
And Jan Levinson

Ripples, ripplets
Rhyming couplets
Skipping across the lake.
Breaking into waves
As the wind takes
Hold and slips and curls
Upon itself, boldly rushing
Brushing into white spume ---
Spins and twirls unfurling
Into pianissimo, slow, slowly
Making room - space - release
For a few moments of grace and peace.

David Talbot 26/7/15

Kismet

I should hate
Everything being left to Fate
- No Mind!
Everything is predestined.
Whatever I did
Was already thought out by SID.
Silly Idiotic Destiny.

What is the point
Everything would be out of joint
There would be no reason for treason
And why have a winter season?
What is the point of being cold
Unless you are VERY old
Dead - coffin lined with lead.
What is the point of carrying on
When we know where we have gone?
I suppose it is quite obscene
Knowing where we've actually been.

I turn the page
And realise it's been quite the rage
To know
Where we are about to go.
Christianity I can forgive
But - FATE!
Please let us live.
I lie
It would be simpler to die,
But knowing fate
I would probably end up late!!

Obituary or rather a Fatality -
A maturation of a of a lifetimes thought
That has eventually come to nought.
18/2/2000 D.Talbot.

La Mer

Wave and wash swirl and lisp.
Seething hiss of swan-white froth.
Crest, crisp, curling,
Towering rage
Sweeping down trough of bitterness
Plunge down repugnant up heave
Of self. Got lost in messy self pity.
One wave, one wonderful
Joyous uplift aloft.
Tip and topple into pit of self seethe.
Lift and fall, lift and fall.
Wave and wash upon wave and wash
Wash
Wash clean, clean

David Talbot

Lady Alicia's Bathroom Song

Listen .... Listen ......
Listen to the rain .....
Singing on the window-pane.
Listen ... . Listen ....
Listen to the Rain ....
Gurgling down the Gutter
Gushing down the drain.
Little Drops joining
All together
Adding up to a spell
Of really bad weather.
Listen .... Listen ....
Listen to the wind.
Whistling, howling,
Rattleing the bins.
Watching the washing
Embodied by the Wind
Filling out Blouses, shirts and things.
Pitter-Patter puddle-patterns.
Dancing Sound.
Ducks and Drakes all lakeing around.
Listen .. Listen ..
Glistening drops
As the Sun comes out
The Raining stops.
D.Talbot Dec 27/28 - 03

Magic

It was so quiet
You could hear stars
Twinkling like crystal-frost
On Christmas trees in the Forest.
Snow hushing cushioning
- Crushing sound into silence.
Icicles hanging - dangling like Damocles sword
Cutting the umbilical cord
As noiseless as the footsteps of deer
Unheard. Only hoof prints left as evidence
Of their passing - Nothing stirred.
You could hear yourself think
Brain whirring - soft as down on an owl's wing
- Singing lullabies as sweet as babies sleeping.

You could hear Christmas coming
As quiet as children creeping down the stair
Staring – amazed – daring – dazed
In open-eyed surprise – delight
At what has happened on Christmas night.
It goes to show
As silent – as beautiful
As the coming of the snow.

D.Talbot 18/8/05

Mothersday Idyll

Wumps was wandering through the forest looking for a florist.

It was Wumpersday and on Wumpersday it was expected of Little Wumps to give things like Chocies, Flowers and Pressies to their Wumper.

Suddenly - before Little Wumps there lay a carpet of Bluebells - "Oh! - How

beautiful" - she cried - "Hours of Flowers", she bathed in their beauty -

Rolly-Pollyed in their glory - Dwelt in their smell - Roamed in the aroma -

captured the spirit, became the sprite of bluebell wood forever. It was in her soul. She became an integral part of the wood.

By the time she arrived home the few flowers that were left clasped in her hand were limp and conveyed none of the beauty that she had seen and felt. Gone was the glory - No royal-blue carpet for her Queen to walk on - just a few wilted bluebells. Crestfallen - Dismayed - Clutching at the fragments of memory of the wood - she whispered "But Wumper, you should have seen them - these are but a poor remembrance -an apology". the moment had gone.

Little Wumps never forgot the beauty she had seen and felt that day beneath the spring-green-leafed boughs and branches. It was a beauty that was - well - not quite impossible to give - but - difficult - very difficult. It was something that imbued her whole being. It was the depth and deepness that shone out from her eyes. It was the sparkle of dew that glistened there -

How was Little Wumps to know that she was so blessed (or perhaps cursed

by the wood).That plucking a little of it - to give its intrinsic beauty was to destroy the very thing she held, spellbound. To be - for a moment only - but part of her forever.

It is strange - but some would trample across this carpet and admire their footprints in the crushed stems and petals as if it was a barren beach that the next tide would wash clean and leave no trace of their desecration. Perhaps they are unaware that others share the confines of our planets space.

I can only say that Little Wumps haunts the woods and places where few go - perhaps because they are afraid to be alone, and when they are they have to leave their mark - So much for the human-race, a disgrace.

D.Talbot 11/4/2000

Railway Walk

(Calder Pit)
Trees arched.
Branch-line bridge-structures.
Dark - Under
Tunnelled - Buried -
Berried - Black and Elder.
Guelder-Rose and willow slender.
Fungii-trunk - Moth-mottled.
Bottle-Green moss on silver-birch bark.
Iron track - mole-muffled
Among sleepered trucks trundling
Ghosts along the Line
Into the dark dank colliered mine
Full of nooks and awkward crannies.
Pick-axe clanging - lights a-dazzle
The whole picture - creating coal -
Within the stricture of the pit.
Candle-lit - Lack of space,
Charcoal-sketches - etched coal face,
Creates the lost subterranean race.
Miners - Past
Yet ever present
As you slowly stroll along the Walk
Toward the coal.

Coming back - the stony way -
They dissappear - at last
Daylight - casting shadows
That are your own.
D.Talbot 13/10/04

To Helen

Mediterranean sun stuns like a dart
So that I cannot see the meditations of my heart.
Before my eyes rises ancient Greece
Whose works of art brought moments of peace.
The image of Helen of Troy silhouetted against the sun
Destroys platonic thoughts.
Oh why can't the two be one?
The dance, the music, the singing;
The longing in the siren's song,
Like the stringing of a violin;
So strong it twines about you,
Grows like a yearning from within,
'till it breaks the bow and sleep seeps in.
Like the sea sleep sweeps in on the beaches of the mind
'till at last you are drawn into the deep beyond dream.

At ebb-tide you find the debris scattered
Like the screaming cry of a gull
Seeking for manna in an empty sun-bleached skull.
Deserted save for the ripple-pattern in the sand
Where waves lisped like thoughts
On the brink of the brain.
Leaving a lasting impression, meek and true;
Not a certain knowledge, a rock to cling to
Oh No! Just a half-heard whisper
Like wind awakening in the branches of the trees
Or an echo from out the blue night sky -
A star sighing down the blackness of the past
And with a roar you wake
Like water battering against the shores of time
And with a start you realise that you have to live
And the only way is to give
Your heart.

David Talbot

The Posh Lady

Dedicated to Sheila

She puts on her face in the morning
Like the sun adorning the day.
A little smile to herself in the mirror
And then - Let's get on with the play.
The plot has already been written
The parts are already cast
So let's get on with today
And try and wipe out the past.

Meanwhile
A clown changes a frown to a smile
The awaiting crowds to beguile
With fun and laughter
And happiness ever after!?
Oh if life was ever so.
The harsh reality just goes to show
That life is tough - rough
Enough to make some people say enough
And others to say whoa! Oh woe!

One thing about the British race
Is that they know how to put on a brave face
But oh! By gosh!
You don't know what it takes to being posh.

Dave Talbot 29th Dec 2013

The Black (K) Night

Literally a bit of doggerel

Robert Le Noir was a knight so bald
He wore a helmet to keep out the cold.
It was when he heard the dragon's roar
His hair fell out onto the floor.
Although he was obviously terrified
He fought the dragon until it died.
For this display of courage he was knighted
And many a maiden he delighted
With acts of valour, bravery and might.
He took up challenges no matter how trite.
Damsels in distress became his forte
As long as they were under forty.

He went on a crusade to the holy lands
But never got farther than Morecombe Sands.
Taking a short cut across the bay
Unfortunately he lost his way.
It wasn't the only thing that he lost
He lost his wagons to his cost
In fact he lost everything!
So he asked for a grant from the King.
The King said "yes" but only if you find The Holy Grail
A Quest our knight dare not fail.
Our errant knight
Disappeared into the blackest night.
He has never been seen ever again.
Robert 'Le Noir' became his name.

A tale is told and it's up to you
Whether you believe it to be true.
On a night that was storming – black as Sin –
A loud knock was heard on the door of an Inn

A serving wench answered, to let them in
And there stood a knight drenched through to the skin.
He said "give me victuals and horses new
And a flagon of your finest brew".
He settled himself in front of the fire
Hoping to get a little drier.
Eventually off came his helmet
He hung it on the nearest pelmet.
Everyone could see he was as bald-as-a-coot
As he sat there in his rusty old suit.
He scoffed his food and quaffed his ale
Then began to tell them a wondrous tale
How he rescued a damsel in distress
Cornered by a fire-dragon - no less.
He said that was how he lost his hair
Rescuing that damsel 'Oh so Fair'.
Although he was burning with desire
It was his hair that set on fire.
So on and so forth he told many a feat
He had accomplished and the foes he did beat
That when it came time for him to leave
They all began to really grieve.
The serving wench said "Sire you cannot depart
Because I love you with all my heart",
But he insisted he had to go
Even though it had begun to snow.
Fresh horses just could not be found
All they could find was a Newfoundland hound.
As the door opened, she gave him a farewell kiss
But he said "You cannot turn a knight out on a dog like this"
Which created loads of laughter
And they all lived happily ever after.

D.Talbot 25/6/12

Tantrum Dance

Feet stamp, beat.
High pitched shriek,
Hands clench, teeth bite
Tight together, white pillars of wrath
With Samson wrenching for release.
All violence braced, crash and fight
Fling annoying toy away.
Path to peace.
Real-life to playful impudent prance.
Wild scream slows to dreamlike whimper.
Temper simpers down with a hiss
Like steam escaping from a kettle.
Battle-frown to gentle grace and charm.
Smile all meek and holy
As only a child can be
In your arms.

David Talbot

The Aardvark

Common name Anteater
Length about half-a-metre.
It's long snout
Is for rooting out
Ants It's favourite diet.
It's best routine is just keeping quiet
Waiting for the ants to come out
Then licks them up an washes 'em down
With a bottle of stout.
Unfortunately he burst out with carbuncles
So now he sticks to eating only uncles.

David Talbot 10/2/14

Night And Day

(For Jackie's peace of mind)
The Park is Peaceful
Except for children playing
Delaying my repose.
Recalling my childhood days
Within the Sanctuary of the park. Those
Were precious days - Rollypollying down the hill.
The hill was but a little mound
Upon which was mounted an anti-aircraft gun.
We still had lots of fun, running, playing tig as children do.
We found out that war had just begun
But couldn't understand the ballyhoo.
I trapped a bee in a snapdragon; the sting still brings tears to my eyes
The one thing about life is
It is still full of surprises.
Antirrhinum Delirium.
Happy days - and later on taking
My own children recreating
Pushing prams, roundabouts and swings
Building sandcastles - doing lots of lovely things.
The flower-beds and rose-beds beautifully kept
The bowling-green close mown, the pathways well swept.
In the midst of which we find
The sun-dial - which was always an hour behind.
Slowly, surely, sitting in the sun
I am dreaming of days before time began.
Sleep comes peacefully to those
Who can let go of life's woes.
Yes I suppose I owe a lot to the park -
But you won't find me there after dark!

David Talbot 1/7/13

Ode To Anne

Water flows under the bridge
Like the passage of time.
A game of Pooh-Sticks.
It depends on the flow
Which way to go.
We may end up in a trickle
Or get swept away
Along the mainstream of life
Not knowing where we are going.
Sometimes the backwater
Gives us time to realise
That we have arrived and can dwell
In the beauty around us
And be ourselves.

Listening to the music of life
Evolving around us
Like the fluting of a fife
Sounding out new ways of growing
into knowing who we are
And with a tremor of fear
Why we are here.

David Talbot. 9 - 15 /8/16

Ode To Brubeck

Blue shadows in the street.

The Moon glows along an empty street
Throwing shadow-patterns
Lunar fantasy - complete contrast -
Silhouetted cameo figures, lingering, longing.
Lonely blue-moon lantern
Illuminating litter cast aside -
Scattered debris of the mindless
Careless trash - splashed across the street.
Visual imagery reflecting
The tinkle of cans - wind-blown -
Adding sound - an inkling -
Profound music - blues -
Deep blue hues flowing into darkness
And becoming shadow-like
Blue shadows dancing along the street.
Rhythm and beat, tinkling pianissimo
Disappearing into a twinkling, star-lit empty sky
Allowing us to ponder
And wonder ... why?

Dave Talbot
29/4/15 - 19/8/15

Parental Responibility

Dear Mum
You gave me life
And above all else
You chose my Dad.
Dear Dad
I learnt from you
How to know Good from Bad
Best lesson I've ever had
And eee! - By gum!
Thank god you chose my Mum.
I thank you both with all my heart
In Life -- I couldn't have had a better start.
Now that you have both passed on
Will I be able to hand it on?

David Talbot 7/2/14

Philosophy - Ode To Keats

Dear Mary I dedicate this poem to you.
The controversial ending to Keats's Ode to a Grecian Urn
"Beauty is truth —truth beauty - that is all ye know on earth
And all ye need to know." Led to a beautiful discourse between us.
I do recall a lot of it was not even spoken. Perhaps now that is all we
    need
To know -

Truth can be beautiful
It can also be brutal.
Beauty can be truthful
It can also be deceptive.
Truth is an absolute;
Beauty is in the eye of the beholder.
Beauty is a conception.
Truth beauty - beauty truth?
Makes you think!

David Talbot 22/12/15

Rebirth

A rift in the limestone rock
Turns the slow trickling brook
Into a spinning splashing beauteous thing,
Singing into the dream of a deep pool
Where in cool water a speckled trout
Leaps out in a loop of diamond drops.

Aloft in the ash-boughs embrace
The soft cooing of doves
Carries the symbol of peace.

A gap in the great forests foliage
Allows a flame of sun fire
Into the dense green undergrowth,
Then back into the soft light loveliness
Of green leaves, lichens and moss.

A day gone by in the birdsong of nature
At the pure beginning of things.
Now, back into the loud darkness of the town
Into the crowded camp of the civilised herd.
Oh! Let there be light,
'Let there be light'.
But it's practically gone,
Drowned in a dream of darkness
Upon the face of the waters.
Only a raft of rainbow-lit clouds
Adrift on the blue night sky.
A shaft of silver moonlight
Gleaming through long slit shrouds.
A draught of cool evening air
Carrying a dream of rain

And a rustle of leaves for its song.
Only this and the sleep and peace and lack of pain,
And the love-cry of a new born babe.

David talbot

Recipe For Success

The termites mound was heaving
For all the ants were leaving.
A Nile length line
Went out to dine
Following the aroma the wind was weaving.
It led them across the Serengeti
To a yet undiscovered Yeti
Munching his lunch
Of banana by the bunch
Covered in MARMITE and Spaghetti.
D.Talbot 13/3/98

Reflections

Outside the dark park
A bright light shining in the still damp air.
A street lamp sentinel, flickering, hesitant.
Long black shadow-trees, full length flung
Fall silently into a sinister pool of darkness.
Small groups of trees lean and leer,
Secretly murmur to one another, ritualistically.
Sinister ripple upon the still pool of darkness.
Silhouetted trees loom ominous,
Pagan fantasies.
Sculptured crescent moon
Pierces the midnight-blue sky
With a cruel cry of anguish
As Africa - the Dark one
Prepares her sacrifice.

Far away beyond man
Sky-lights - God's stars Illuminate heaven.
Symbolic stars, precious scintillating light
Suspended above the midnight pool of the world.
Perhaps we see the truth about God
In the reflections of the deep pool.
For a moment I am lost in wonder
Which are the more beautiful
Man made sentinel candles or the far flung light of God?
I lift skyward
Reach for the stars of my first knowledge
And know which is the original - consequently the image.
For from man emits a hesitant flicker of creation
A reflection.

The earth stars blink back a remorseful message
And at last the moon sleeps in a mystical twilight
Akin to the half perception of man

Surrounded by a world of twilight, starlight
And the shadow lilt of lamplight,
Whilst the black men of the Dark one
Still beat the naked drum

Dave Talbot

Reflected In The Window Pane

I remember as a child travelling by train.
The wild shriek of steam escaping - as if in pain.
The pistons gleaming in and out
The shout of people bustling about
the station platform as the train goes out.

Day-dreaming in the window seat
Lulled by the rocking rythym and beat.
The passing clouds in the sky
The telegraph poles whistling by
Measuring distance - I dont know why.
Allows one to forget and then remember
The little things that seemed to matter.
Yet, the chattering track
Seems to bring most things back
- rekindled embers - everythings clear
And then the landscapes become a blur
- where am I? -
Its not easy to see
What really has become of me
And then as the picture clears
revealing the worst of fears
For there its very plain to see
- I wonder what became of Me -
The little boy full of ideas.
Along Life's track and whirring wheels -
The little boy with ideals.

D.Talbot 5/11/99.

Ships Passing In The Night

You came to me in Darkness.
Lighting the night with delight.
Illuminating the fact
That you were something that I lacked.
Joying in good company
Allowing love to kindle into something that I adore.

Then you departed
Leaving me broken hearted
Lonelier than ever before

David Talbot Nov 2014

Siamese Sins

Coco the cat grew so fat
He went rolling instead of climbing
He rolled into church then fell with a lurch
That set the bells all chiming.
The people came and stared in shame
At Coco's misdirection.
The choir boys sang
And with a clang
The parson took collection.

Dave Talbot

Skating On Thin Ice

There is something - in the air
That wasn't there
Before I met you.
We walk ... we hold hands
We talk ... and then just joy
In being together.
Enjoying the grandeur of life.
To be so free from worry -
No need to hurry -
No need to rush,
Nothing pushing us over the edge
Into a pledge that we will regret.
How can we forget those moments?

Yet!
We do.
Rueing those precious moments
Tossed between despair and paradise -
Lost.
To regain that trust takes time
But we must
Open arms and welcome
Each others charms
As if nothing had happened.

Dave Talbot 28/2/15

Sleeping Indian

Dedicated to Jackson Hole
And Jan Levinson

Hiawatha we shall find you
Sleeping high upon the Mountains.
Dreaming of dear Minnehaha
Dancing naked in the fountains.
Sunlight splashing all around you
Awakening memories - Oh! So sweet.
The moment that you first saw her
Really swept you off your feet.
So you lie there dreaming
Of peace and plenty,
Remembering when everything was empty.
The days of dancing round the cornfields
So that they will yield more harvest
So that your people will not starve.
Hoping that the beasts around you
Breed and multiply
So that there is meat to carve.

A simple people enjoying life
As it should be lived.
I wonder why?
Can white-mans coming be forgiven?
So sleep you brave
You have what we crave
Peace of mind - a way of living
To be joyed in,
That we have destroyed.
In retrospect, looking back
You had what white-man lacked.
Respect - for those around you,
Reliance on each other - sister - brother.

So sleep on and dream
Of the day that we can come together
And realise as I do
That sometimes dreams can come true.
Let us smoke a pipe of peace together
And make sure our people will live forever
In the security of the mountains
Where you sleep in deep repose.
We shall look up to you and find
A kind of loveliness as delicate
And as beautiful as a rose.

David Talbot 26/7/15

The Dreamer

(Dear Anne - Thank you for your Good Company)

Leprechauns, Unicorns, Satyrs and Fauns
Dancing and prancing across the lawns,
Swathed in Irelands shamrock-green,
Courting, cavorting, quite unseen
Except by those that chose
To dream.
Legends, Myths and Fairytales
Enchant the Past.
With things that could never last.
We hear, we listen
But do we believe
That these things ever occurred?
Things that seem quite absurd
Yet, let's not forget
Folklore came from times before Today
Thank Goodness for this delay.
Make-believe might deceive
But what is handed down
Through Minstrel's, Dancing, Arts and Craft
Is far better than an overdraft.
There are things in life
You cannot borrow
Like tomorrow - to my sorrow
You cannot bank
On it or thank
Or look back
To find things that you lack.
It Makes you scream!

Sometimes I think it wise
To Blink and simply close your eyes
And dream.

David Talbot 11/3/16

Splat

I saw him in the morning
Roaming in the hedgerow,
Scuttling around and into the field
Hiding under scarecrow.
His eyes were bright and full of life
Probably off to find a wife
Who knows?

I found him in the evening
That's the way life goes
SPLAT!
And that is that.
One little hedgehog laid out flat
Apart from his little nose.
By David Talbot
25/5/93

Striding On With Pride

Technique is something you acquire or learn.
I t is possible that a genius could teach -
But you can't teach genius.
Self-satisfaction can lead to better things
Like a young bird singing
And then taking wing.
Bringing one to realize
Skies' the limit.
Sing like a linnet
And soar above
Momentary upsets.
Don't forget
Just paint with love.

David Talbot 8/7/16

Summer Snow

The willow weeps its seeds.
Light wisps of whiteness
Heeding the vagaries of the breeze
Drifting into hollows where some may grow.
Rose-bay-willow-herb
Colouring the moors with its rose-red hue.
Casting forth snowflakes
Linking Lancashire and Yorkshire
A mixture of roses.
Peace at last.

David Talbot 12/7/14

Talent

(A tribute to Tina's abilities)

I see -
Something in the sky-blue sea
That seems like part of me.
Dreams drifting by, cloud-high.
I wonder why?
Sea-blue, ultra-marine
With perhaps a tinge of green,
Carries me into peaceful calm.
Balmy breezes drift and flow -
Growing - allowing me to know
That going into this space
Fills me with awe and grace.
It's like being drawn into another world
As if the beginning of life has been unfurled.
I see?

(Skies so blue, red roses too
Here am I and there are you
And I said to myself
What a wonderful world.)

David Talbot 9/2/16

The Magic Of Christmas

Father Christmas slid down the chimney
All covered in soot and grime.
He thought to himself this delivering
Toys at Christmas is a right pantomime.
Once a year I've got to slim
In order that I can climb
The going down is easy
Its getting back up again that takes time.
Still I suppose someone's got to do it
Just think – no goodies on Christmas morning
There'd be one heck of a stink!
Children's faces would drop down in disappointment.
Anticipation squashed down to nothing.
Parent's faces all in the pink.
No I couldn't let that happen
I couldn't let them down
The spirit of Christmas has got to be preserved
So each year I don my red gown
And come up with things that they have deserved.
So dear children on Christmas morn
When you open your presents be thankful
That you were born into a family that cares for you
And - dare I say it? Please be aware
That you are the lucky ones.
Some of these modern houses
Are beyond recall - they have no chimneys
So the children living in them
Get nothing at all!
Dear children in chimneyless houses
As you are opening your presents
What I said before could have been tragic
But - if you have presents to open
Well - that's Magic!

David Talbot 24/4/14

The Mystical Wind

Peaceful sound of sea
In wind, tree, clouds.
Proud and peaceful Wind beech trees
High and heavenly clean white wisp-clouds
And Pendle towering in a mist of peace.

Loud wind winding and sighing in the beech-bough leaves
Fluttering and uttering a half-heard birdsong sigh
In the stutter and stagger of the beast in the wind.
Half-heard in the happy looping wavelets
I say half-heard, the rest lost
In the roar and rave of the beast in the wind.

David talbot

Under Willow Trees In Summer

Soft whimmering of wings.
A humming-bird-hued dragonfly
Hovers, like a humble bee
Above full flowering iris's.
Fleeting shadow, like a cloud of sunset.
Swallows on strumming wings
Swing under eaves for shelter.
Deep murmur of rain on leaves and grass
Soft deep vibrations of passing showers.
A trembling stem of wheat in the field,
Bends, yields its slender strength
In a graceful quivering curve
As a nervous harvest mouse,
Sleek and trembling,
Climbs, Clings precariously.
Clean lissom body,
Gold reflecting dark eyes
In gleaming sun and golden ears of corn,
Rippling in soft breezes.
Quiet whispering of birds.
Fluttering, lisping willow leaves
Wavering in impulsive wind.
Rustling, rippling yellow wheat waves
Tossing in shimmering summer heat
Beneath a cloud speckled blue sky.

Eyes all sparkling with life,
Lips tremulous with unspoken words,
Yearning heart, trembling in love
Pressed close to mine.

Soft whimmering of wings.

David Talbot

What Is Love

The bonding of bodies
Creating life.
The giving of self for another.
Accepting someone as a wife.
Believing in someone as a brother.
Supporting in the midst of strife.
Becoming a mother.
Giving - to create a better world.
Giving - not expecting anything in return.
A yearning - a want - a need to believe
Not knowing what you believe in!
Just to BE. Beloved.
To love
To give of oneself. Lets' get real
What is love? I can't tell you
It is something that you feel.

David Talbot 22/1/13

Lightning Source UK Ltd.
Milton Keynes UK
UKOW01f1228071216

289343UK00003B/471/P